OMG Dad's Cooking

By Eran Iohan

Your Everyday Healthy and Easy Recipes Cookbook

Printed in the United States of
America

First Printing, 2014

ISBN-13: 978-1500356149
ISBN-10: 150035614X

omgdadscooking@gmail.com

to my love, my best friend, my wife...Gili

About this Book

First thing First

Take a pen and cross-off the word "Your" on the cover and the first page. Write your name instead. This is your cooking book, make it yours.

Simplicity

This cookbook is all about simplicity. The book is designed for those who are not novices chefs, rather for those that often find themselves avoiding standing in the kitchen preparing a meal.

The Internet is full of recipes of every cuisine on earth. But where to start looking for those simple, bullet proof cuisines is not an easy task. That is why the recipes here are very easy, short and include very clear cooking instructions without any chefs lingo.

This cookbook in actually a cooking notebook, it doesn't have chromo pages or fancy pictures. It is designed as a notebook with a real purpose for you to write in it (and I encourage you to do so). Add tips to each recipe, I left room for that, correct the oven temperature to your oven at home for best results or just cross out and write anything you have experienced with and made the recipe better and tastier for your family and guests.

I personally also believe that good, everyday home food should be simple and will not require rare or expensive ingredients. You will be able to find all the ingredients in this book in your local neighborhood grocery store. As a matter of fact, you probably have most of the items in your kitchen already.

Good for the Family

When I decided to collect those recipes to a book, my intension was to get the recipes my family loves and asks me to make again and again. Kids (or maybe just mine) are tough crowd. First, they must see what they eat. The dishes must be separately visible on the plate or the table. Second they like simple, plain or unblended flavors. Third and most importantly they will eat it if it tastes good, and they will tell you right in your face what they think about it.

On top of all that, each family has its own craziness around food. My daughters don't like to see leaves inside their food. So no parsley, thyme or coriander (god forbid). Others avoid dairy or meat. It's all good, I'm certain you will find what you and your family like in this book.

The book is divided into weekdays and weekends recipes. I know from firsthand experience that for families weekdays feel like a roller-coasters and time for preparing lunch or dinner is very limited and food served should be comforting. So weekdays pieces are quick and effortless. On the weekends you probably can spend more time cooking, but I guessed you would like to spend it doing something else with your family. So weekends recipes are little more complex but don't require much longer cooking time.

Recipes in this book are all based on personal family experience. So they are all good for serving 4-6 people, and none taste spicy hot. As always, you know better what works for your audience, so adjust accordingly.

Healthy Food

My motto for cooking at home is that it has to be nutritious food. There are plenty of unhealthy food you can order in or heat-up from your freezer. If you already considered preparing a meal at home whether to your family or guests, and picked up this selection of recipes, make an effort keep it healthy.

Healthy food also means to know the ingredients that make up my food. I like to season my bread crumbs, prepare tomato sauce or making rice with type of lentils of my choice. All of those can be bought ready to use in the store, it saves time no doubt but you can't always be sure what's in the box. Same goes with organic food. You decide.

With all the research that is done around the world about obesity and the type of food we consume, for my family sake I make an effort and avoid cooking with butter or deep fried food, I use good quality olive oil and try as many as possible different color vegetables and pulses. Meat recipes in this book will welcome leaner meats like turkey or chicken.

Although the book was originally addressed for Dads, I intentionally avoided the grilling routine for the following two reasons. First, almost every guy I know has his own theory around how to perfect the grill. Second, I try keeping grilling to a minimum so this book is all about other choices.

Versatile

The recipes in this book are definitely uncomplicated, but it doesn't mean you can't take it to the next level. Recipes are a starting point for the cook to experience. Explore adding ingredients to or excluding them from your cooking. You can replace and get a totally different flavor or look. If something works well, write it inside so you have it for next time. Make this book your own personal cooking book.

Many cookbooks include instructions how to serve the food that was just cooked. All the cuisines you make from this book are great serving as family style. But if you are cooking for guests or for your important other you can always serve it in individual plates and garnish. Be creative.

Enjoy

The most important element, enjoy making food to your love ones and enjoy watching them eat your creation. Have fun.

Some recipes are so simple your kids can help out or make them on their own, they will enjoy the credits at the table.

Share

Reviews (good or bad), comments and any great ideas, are most welcome.
Share with me at: omgdadscooking@gmail.com

Weekdays

Breaded Chicken Tenders

This is the Holy Grill of food for kids. If given a choice they would pick this every day of the week. So mastering the secrets of good chicken tenders are a must for every parent.

What you need:

6-8 chicken cutlets
2 cups plain bread crumbs
1/2 cup flour
2 eggs
1 tsp paprika
1/4 tsp turmeric (for color)
salt and pepper

Seasoning add-on to the bread crumbs can be cumin, sesame seeds, thyme, oregano and more

While frying the entire cutlet surface is in contact with the pan.

What you need to do:

- in a bowl large enough to hold 2 cutlets, beat the eggs.
- in a similar size bowl, add bread crumbs and seasoning. mix well until the mixture looks uniform.
- using a paper towel, dry out the cutlets.
- powder the cutlets with flour. shake to remove any access flour.
- heat a pan over medium heat. pour cooking oil so that you will have 1/8 inch (3 mm) of oil in the pan.
- dip cutlets in the eggs' bowl. make sure they are completely covered with beaten eggs.
- remove and place cutlets in the bread crumbs mixture, again make sure they are well covered with bread crumbs.
- place the breaded cutlets into the hot pan (no more than 2-4 at a time). careful the oil is HOT place them in the pan away from you.
- fry the cutlets on one side, until golden brown about 2 min. flip to the other side.
  remove from pan onto a plate or a baking dish covered with paper towel to absorb access oil.

Adjust the heat so the bread crumbs don't burn too quickly if it's too hot, or get oily if it's too low

Meat Saucers

These delicious flying saucers are best eaten right from the pan. Avoid making extra for the next day, they will not taste as good (like eggrolls from two days ago).

What you need:

1 lb (1/2 kg) ground meat
1 medium onion
1 clove of garlic
1 egg
1 Tbsp olive oil
3 Tbsp plain bread crumbs
1 tsp paprika
1/4 tsp turmeric (for color)
salt and pepper

What you need to do:

- grate onion and garlic (or just use a food processor) into a mixing bowl. discard some of the onion liquids. add the rest of the meat balls ingredients and mix it all together. let rest covered for 1/2 an hour.
- prepare about 10-12 meat balls and flatten them a little (should look like a flying saucer).
- heat a pan with 3 Tbsp of cooking oil, fry about 3-4 saucers at a time until brown on both sides. remove and place them on a paper towel. repeat until all saucers are fried (add oil as necessary).

Work very well with combination of turkey and meat

Meat Balls in Red Sauce

Hello !! someone said comfort food.
Serving these meat balls right from the pot on top mashed potatoes or rice is a sheer delight. Of course if this is meatless day today, the sauce itself is a perfect match for Farfalle pasta.

What you need:

Meat balls:
1 lb (1/2 kg) ground meat
1 large onion
1 clove of garlic
1 egg
1 Tbsp olive oil
1 Tbsp bread crumbs
1 tsp paprika
1/4 tsp turmeric (for color)
salt and pepper

Red sauce:
2 Tbsp cooking oil
1 cup crashed tomatoes
6 Tbsp tomatoes paste
1 medium carrot, diced small
1 large onion, diced small
2 stems of celery, diced small
1 medium potato, diced small
1 cloves of garlic, sliced thin
1/2 tsp chili pepper flakes
1/2 tsp sugar
2 cups water, boiling
salt and pepper

Any type of meat or combination will work. Adjust oil and bread crumbs quantities

Parsley, oregano and/or coriander are welcome in the last minute into the sauce

What you need to do:

- grate onion and garlic (or just use the food processor) into a mixing bowl. add the rest of the meat balls ingredients and mix it all together. let rest covered in the fridge for 1/2 an hour.
- in a dutch oven or a saute pan, saute the sauce onions until golden. add the garlic and chili pepper and stir for 1 min.
- add carrots, celery and the potato and saute for 2-3 minutes.
- add tomatoes sauce, paste and sugar and stir for 1 min. add water, salt and pepper. bring to a boil, lower the heat and simmer for 10 min.
- make 12-18 golf ball size meat balls, and add to the sauce. simmer for 30 min.

Cook meat balls on a light simmer or they will break into the sauce

Rice, Chicken and Apple

Look, there is always something to do with tasteful roasted chicken (check page 30). Here is a great example that doesn't require much of cooking, perfect for weekdays as it makes a whole meal in one bowl.

What you need:

1/4 roasted chicken
2 cups cooked rice
1/2 Granny Smith apple
1/4 cup scallion, sliced
vinaigrette dressing (p. 17)
salt and pepper

Use only tart apples. Other kind of apples make this dish too sweet

Try it.

What you need to do:

- place rice in a large bowl.
- take chicken meat apart, into small bite size pieces. add to the bowl.
- slice the apple as thin as possible, then cut the slices into smaller pieces at the size of the meat. add to the bowl
- add scallion
- pour the vinaigrette into the bowl. mix well. taste. add salt and pepper as needed.

Any fresh green leaves will be nice like parsley, oregano or thyme.
Small amounts of sage or coriander will also be great.

Try it also.

Roasted Root Vegetables

One of the best ways to eat verity of vegetables, is to roast them all together like one big happy family. For best results - high heat, short oven time and minimal seasoning.

What you need:

3-4 carrots cut loose
2-3 potatoes cubed to six
1 yam cubed to six
2 snips cut loose
3 Tbsp vegetable oil
1 Tbsp paprika
1/2 tsp chili flakes
1 tsp salt
1/2 tsp pepper
1/4 tsp sugar

Beats are also great roasted. Beats must be mixed separately with oil and seasoning. Otherwise all veggies will be red

What you need to do:

- preheat the oven to 400F (200C).
- drop all vegetables into a mixing bowl, add oil and mix, coating all veggies.
- add seasoning and mix well (for best results use your hands), so that all vegetables are well coated with oil and seasoning.
- place in a baking dish covered with parchment paper and bake for about 40-60 min.

MAKE A WHOLE MEAL

Place drumsticks and thighs in a Ziploc bag. Add the same seasoning (without the sugar). Place in a 380F (190C) oven for 40 min.

Forked Mashed Potatoes

There are probably hundreds of mashed potatoes recipes, but I like this one because it is that simple. The rough finish gives it a home touch, and at the table everyone fights over the chunks.

What you need:

6-7 medium size potatoes
1/4 cup milk
salt and pepper

Milk can be replaces with 3 Tbsp of Olive oil.

What you need to do:

- peel the potatoes. cut them so that all pieces are about the same size (don't cut any smaller than quarters).
- place the potatoes in a pot, cover with cold water then and 2 inches (5 cm) more.
- bring water to a boil, once boiled add about 1Tbsp of salt.
- cook for 7-10 min until the potatoes easily slide off a knife stuck into the middle of the piece.
- remove the cooking water, leave in the pot about 1/4 cup of the cooking water. let the pot sit for 5 min for the potatoes to cool down.
- mash the potatoes with a fork, chunks are very welcome. make sure no water are left at the bottom of the pot.
- warm up the milk in the microwave. it must be HOT. stir it into the pot.
- add salt and pepper as needed.

Couscous Salad

Colorful and tasteful salad. It will be a great addition to any meal. As always you can mix and match to fit your palate.

Couscous is a great side dish to any meal. Try it with Veggies cooked for 15-20 min in chicken broth.

To have a yellow couscous, add 1/4 tsp of turmeric to the dry couscous.

What you need:

1 lb (1/2 kg) whole wheat instant couscous
3 cups boiling water
2-3 carrots
1 cucumber
6 Tbsp olive oil
1/2 lemon
1 tsp apple vinegar
1 tsp salt
Pinch pepper

Cucumbers can be replaced with Almonds and/or Walnuts

Add 1/2 cup of chopped parsley and some coriander, for fresher taste

What you need to do:

- in a large mixing bowl, place the dry couscous and 3 Tbsp of olive oil. mix well using a fork.
- add boiling water. stir well. cover and let rest for 10-15 min.
- add to the mixing bowl, carrots and cucumber, lemon juice, vinegar, salt and pepper and 3 Tbsp of olive oil.
- mix well, fluffing the couscous using a fork.
- place in the fridge for flavors to blend for at least two hours.

Green Salad with Honey Vinaigrette

Simple, Simple, Simple.
Check the tips on this page for many twists and additions, or you can explore others ideas yourself.

What you need:

1 romaine lattice
1 cup baby greens
2-3 carrots

Use and mix different kinds of lattice and greens.

Vinaigrette:
2 1/2 Tbsp olive oil
1/2 lemon
1 tsp apple vinegar
1 Tbsp honey
1/2 tsp salt
Pinch pepper

What you need to do:

- cut the lattice into 1/2 inch (1 cm) wide strips. place in a mixing bowl.
- add the baby greens
- peel the carrots. using the peeler continue to shave long strips from all sides until you reach the carrot core. cut the length of the strips to match those of the lattice.
- squeeze the half lemon into a small jar with a lid (remove pits). add vinegar, honey, salt and pepper. add the olive oil. close the lid and shake well until all ingredients combine (mainly the honey). open and taste, correct seasoning.
- just before serving add 2/3 of the vinaigrette into the mixing bowl. toss lightly until all leave and carrots are lightly covered. taste. add dressing if needed.

Vinaigrettes

Vinaigrettes can come is endless flavors and colors:
*   * use Balsamic Vinegar*
*   * switch to orange juice (no need to add sugar or honey)*
*   * add fresh thyme or oregano*

Rice & ...

Rice and lentils make a complete meal of protein and carbs. So I cherish this combination dearly. Below are merely two examples how to make rice into a feast of flavors and colors.

... Green Lentils and Onion

What you need:

1/2 cup green lentils
1 cup rice
1 large onion diced
1 clove of garlic minced
 1/2 tsp cumin
salt and pepper

Black or Pearl lentils can be used as well. Adjust cooking time accordingly.

What you need to do:

- saute the onion in the cooking pot until golden brown. remove from the put.
- put lentils, cumin and garlic into the pot. cover with water and an inch (2-3 cm) more. bring to a boil and lower the heat to a simmer. cook for 15-20 min. until lentils are soft with a bite.
- add rice, onion and a pinch of salt and pepper. add water as needed. bring to a boil. stir. cover and move the pot to the smallest burner and reduce heat to the minimum.
- cook for 12-15 min. remove from the stove and keep the pot covered for 5 min. more.

.... Peas, Orange Lentils and Carrots

What you need:

1/4 cup orange lentils
1 cup rice
1 large onion, diced small
2 cloves of garlic, sliced thin
1/2 cup sweet peas
1/2 cup carrots, diced small
2 Tbsp olive oil
salt and pepper

Brown rice time is much longer, consider that when using it with other veggies.
Carrots and lentils are OK, softer veggies might not taste as good after a long simmer.

What you need to do:

- saute the onions in the cooking pot until translucent. add garlic and stir for 1 min. (don't let it burn).
- add sweet peas and carrots, saute for 2-3 min.
- add lentils and rice to the pot. stir for 1 min. add water as needed. cover. bring to a boil. stir and cover. move the pot to the smallest burner reduce heat to a minimum.
- cook for about 12-15 min. remove from stove and let the pot sit covered for 5 min. more.

Roasted Cauliflower

I know there are diverse opinions about cauliflower. Once you try this super easy recipe you will embrace it forever.

What you need:

1 whole Cauliflower with leaves on
3 Tbsp olive oil
salt and pepper

What you need to do:

- preheat the oven to 450F (220C).
- put the whole cauliflower heads down inside a pot full with water. bring to a boil. add 1-1/2 tsp of salt. cook for 10-15 min until the cauliflower leaves get tender.
- strain the water and let the cauliflower cool down a little.
- pour 2 Tbsp of olive oil, rub it all over the white flowers. season with salt and pepper.
- cover baking dish with parchment paper. place the cauliflower inside. bake for 15-20 minutes until golden brown (with some burned spots).
- drip 1 Tbsp of olive oil before serving

Try serving it with sour cream or just plain yogurt.

Bulgur Spoon Salad

This salad is as Mediterranean as food can be. Fresh, full of vegetables, lemon juice and olive oil. The salad can be prepared a little ahead of time, this will enable the bulgur to soak some of the salad wonderful juices.

What you need:

6-7 medium tomatoes
2 medium cucumber
1/2 cup bulgur
1-2 lemons
2 Tbsp olive oil
salt and pepper

What you need to do:

- put the bulgur in a large container, and add 4 cups of room temp. water. let it sit for at least 20 min (the bulgur crumbs should feel edible but still firm).
- cut the tomatoes and cucumbers to small cubes. get all veggies and juices into the salad bowl.
- add juice from 3/4 lemon, olive oil, salt and pepper.
- strain the bulgur. get all access water out by leaving it in the strainer for 5 min. add to the salad bowl. mix well.
- taste, add lemon juice, salt and pepper if necessary.
- keep the salad in the bowl for at least 10 min before serving, so that the bulgur absorbs juices from the salad. mix it again before serving.

Add 1/2 cup of chopped parsley and a touch of mint, to make it extra fresh

Green Soup

Great vegetable soup, and due to its velvety texture there is no need for cream. Two cups from this soup makes a nice small lunch.

What you need:

2 cups frozen sweet peas
3 medium carrots, diced small
1 large onion, diced small
2 celery, diced small
3 medium potatoes, diced small
2 cloves of garlic, sliced thin
4 cups water
2 cups broth (chicken or veggie)
2 Tbsp olive oil
salt and pepper

What you need to do:

- saute the onions until golden. add the garlic and stir for 1 min (don't let the garlic burn).
- add carrots and celery and saute for few minutes.
- add peas and stir in the water and stock. bring the soup to a boil, lower the heat and simmer for 10 min.
- add potatoes. bring to a boil, lower the heat and let simmer for additional 10-15 minutes until all veggies are cooked.
- grind the soup in the pot with a stick blender. taste and add salt and pepper as needed. simmer for additional 5 minutes for all flavors to blend.

Keep a cup of cooked veggies aside before grinding. Add 2 Tbsp to each bowl.

It's fun to find these little colored surprises in the soup

Orange Soup

This soup is fabulous as is. In case you want to bring it to the next level a tablespoon of heavy cream to each bowl and few drops of extra virgin olive oil will do the trick.

What you need:

2 cups squash, diced small
4 medium carrots, diced small
1 large onion, diced small
2 stems of celery, diced small
1 medium potatoes, diced small
2 medium sweet potatoes, diced small
2 cloves of garlic, sliced thin
1 red chili pepper, sliced thin
3 cups water
3 cups stock (chicken or veggie)
2 Tbsp olive oil
salt and pepper

Before grinding keep a cup of Veggies aside.
Place 2 Tbsp in each bowl before serving

What you need to do:

- saute the onions until golden. add the garlic and chili peppers and stir for 1 min (don't let the garlic burn).
- add carrots and celery and saute for few minutes.
- add squash saute for 2-3 min. stir in the water and stock. bring the soup to a boil, lower the heat and simmer for 10 min.
- add potatoes and sweet potatoes. bring to a boil, lower the heat and let simmer for additional 10-15 minutes until all veggies are cooked.
- grind the soup in the pot with a stick blender. taste and add salt and pepper as needed. simmer for additional 5 minutes for all flavors to blend.

notes

Weekends

Shak-shu-ka

My favorite weekend morning (needless to say brunch) treat. Served with thick slices of bread you can dip into the warm sauce. Some like it with yogurt but my preference is homemade tahina.

What you need:

6-8 tomatoes, diced
2 sweet peppers green, red, diced
2-3 cloves of garlic
1 small hot pepper or 1/2 tsp chili flakes
4 eggs
4 Tbsp veggie oil (canola)
1/2 tsp sugar
salt and pepper

To speed the process of hardening the eggs, use a lid. Just don't cover it for more than 2 min.

What you need to do:

- on a medium heat add oil to a pan. add the garlic and saute for couple of minutes, stir it continuously. don't let the garlic burn, reduce heat if necessary.
- increase heat, add sweet peppers and saute for about 2 min.
- add the hot pepper flakes, stir for about 1 min.
- add tomatoes, pinch of sugar and 1/2 tsp of salt. saute for 15 to 20 min on high heat. let the tomatoes break and liquids to almost run out while boiling. add salt and pepper to taste.
- make a hole in the sauce, and break an egg inside. repeat for all eggs. cook until egg-white hardens but yoke is still liquid.

Tahina Recipe:

5 Tbsp raw Tahini
1/2 lemon juice
1/2 cup very cold water
1 clove of garlic, minced
pinch of salt

* mix tahini with 1/4 cup of water. add garlic, lemon juice and salt and mix well

* add water and mix until reaches to the right smooth consistency

Pancake

This is the basic stuff with buttermilk as the twist, which makes the pancakes better than with just plain milk. There are endless add-ons and toppings. I encourage you to try each time something different.

What you need:

1 cup white flour
2 tsp baking powder
2 Tbsp sugar
1 egg
3/4 cup buttermilk
1 tsp real vanilla extract
salt

What you need to do:

- put all dry ingredients in a mixing bowl, add the buttermilk and vanilla extract and mix until smooth and consistent (might need to add some water or milk depends on your flour and buttermilk). place in the fridge for 10 min.
- heat a pan on a medium heat. grease it using oil spray or 1 tsp of oil.
- pour from the mixture into the pan to form a size of the pancake you want. don't make too many at one batch. adjust heat as necessary to avoid the pancakes from burning.
- once bubbles appear at the top flip the pancakes to the other side. cook for 1-2 min.
- remove from the pan and keep warm until serving.
- add oil to the pan as necessary and keep making pancakes until you finish the batter.

French Toast

Favorite for brunches on cold wintery days. Best with a strong espresso on the side.

What you need:

1 loaf of bread, sliced thick
2-3 eggs
2 cups milk
1 tsp real vanilla extract

What you need to do:

- beat the eggs in a bowl large enough for a slice of bread you have to fit in.
- in a separate, same size, bowl add the milk and the vanilla extract.
- heat a skillet on a medium-high burner. add cooking oil or oil spray to coat.
- dip the bread in the milk for 1 second on each side. remove. place immediately into the eggs bowl for 2-3 seconds on each side.
- place two to four slices of bread on the hot skillet and cook until golden brown, flip and cook until golden brown on the other side. remove and keep worm until serving.
- repeat for all slices of bread, might need to add milk, vanilla and eggs.

Discard of bread crust, but keep one side, to prevent the bread from falling apart.

To be really mischievous, use a sweet Challah instead of regular bread.

Don't soak the bread for too long in the milk. It makes the bread too soft inside.

Vegetable Pastry

An impressive opening for a weekend meal. Give it a try if you have the time, your family and guests will be amazed.

What you need:

Pastry:
1 cup flour
1/2 cups olive oil
1/3 cup water
1 tsp salt

Topping:
2 eggplants, sliced thin lengthwise
2 cloves of garlic, chopped
1 onion, sliced thin
4 zucchinis, sliced thin
4 tomatoes, sliced thin
Dozen kalamata olives, chopped
4 Tbsp olive oil
thyme or oregano
salt & pepper

If not everyone at the tables likes part of your topping (e.g. kids and eggplants), place those in one side so you can cut it out when serving.

What you need to do:

- in a large mixing bowl, place all the pastry ingredients (dry first) and form a dough. make a ball and wrap in plastic. place in the fridge for an hour.
- coat a skillet with 2 Tbsp of olive oil, saute onions and garlic. add the eggplants and saute on low heat until they are soft. remove from heat add salt and pepper.
- preheat the oven to 380F (190C).
- sprinkle flour on the countertop, a rolling pin and the pastry ball. roll the dough until 1/2-1/4 inch (1-0.5 cm) thin. Place on a baking sheet covered with parchment paper. using a fork stab the dough.
- spread the eggplants and onion mixture over the pastry.
- on top place the zucchinis and tomatoes, spread over the olives.
- sprinkle thyme, oregano or both on top.
- drizzle 2 Tbsp of olive oil and bake for 30-40 min.

Roast Lemony Chicken[1]

This is our family favorite chicken. My kids can eat this juicy chicken every weekend. Lately one chicken is not enough, so I started making two at a time. There is always something tasty to do with those leftovers the following day.

What will you need:

1 whole chicken about 3lb (1.5 kg)
1 lemon
1 small bunch of parsley
4 branches of rosemary
few branches of thyme
3 scallions
4 Tbsp olive oil
salt and pepper
roasting string

Any fresh herb will be a great addition, like Sage, Oregano and more

Add Potatoes, Yams and cloves of garlic to the pan on the last 40min, for a whole meal right there.

What will you need to do:

- preheat an oven to 430F (220C) with the roasting pan inside.
- separate rosemary and thyme leaves from their stems. chop all greens together. This should yield about half a cup. grind zest from a lemon and add it into the herb cup. add 2 Tbsp of olive oil, salt and pepper. mix it all together.
- separate the chicken breast skin from the meat (start at the bottom work your fingers up), to create two pockets. make one or two cuts across the legs. fill the pockets with about half of the herb mixture and spread the rest all over the chicken and into the drum sticks cuts.
- squeeze half a lemon inside the chicken cavity and leave it inside together with two whole stems of rosemary.
- tie the chicken legs to close the cavity.
- remove the roasting pan from the oven (careful its HOT), add 1-2 Tbsp of oil. place the chicken in the pan breast side down. back to the oven for 10 min.
- reduce the oven to 360F (180C) and rotate the chicken, now breast side up. roast about 3/4-1 hour.

---

[1] Inspired by Jamie Oliver "The Naked Chef"

Mediterranean Chicken

Maybe the most complicated recipe in this book, but believe me it worth the effort. The chicken even taste better the next day, if anything left behind. There is plenty of sauce when cooking this chicken, so it is great over rice, mashed potatoes, cuscus and even pasta.

What you need:

6-8 chicken drumsticks & thighs
1 cup butternut squash, cubes
1/2 lb (250 gr) frozen peas
1/2 cup tomato, cubes
2 sweet potatoes, cubes
2 potatoes, cubes
2 celery, chopped small
2 medium onions, chopped
2 cloves of garlic, thinly sliced

4 carrots, 2 chopped small, 2 chunks
6 Tbsp olive oil
6 oz (170 gr) tomato paste
1/2 tsp hot pepper flakes
1/2 tsp sugar
salt and pepper
chopped parsley for garnish

Use a whole celery root. The stems chopped small, leaves add to the sauce in the last 10min and the root cubed together with the rest of the veggies in the last 20min.

What you need to do:

- season the chicken with salt and pepper.
- add 2Tbsp of veggie oil to a hot large sauté pan (large enough to hold all 6-8 pieces of chicken flat), and brown the chicken on all sides. remove from the pan. leave access oil in the pan.
- add 2Tbsp of veggie oil and saute the onion until translucent. add garlic and hot paper flakes and stir for about two minutes (keep stirring don't let it burn). add the small cubes of carrots and celery. saute for 5 min. add tomato paste and sugar on top stir until all veggies are covered with tomato paste. add tomatoes cubes and saute for additional 2 min.
- make room for the chicken and place them back into the pot.
- add boiling water until chicken pieces are covered. season with salt and pepper. mix and bring the pot to a boiling hot and then lower the heat and let it simmer for 40 min with lid on.
- add all remaining veggies (carrots, sweet potato, potato, squash and peas), bring it back to boiling hot and then reduce heat and let simmer for additional 20 min.
- remove from stove and sprinkle with parsley on top.

Hummus

This is the real thing in a short version. Healthy and tasty without all the preservatives and the excess oil you will find in the store hummus. You will be amazed how easy it is to DIY.

What you need:

2 lb (1 kg) frozen chickpeas
2 gloves of garlic
1/2 cup lemon juice
2/3 cup raw tahina
salt

What you need to do:

- in a large pot, place the frozen chickpeas and garlic. cover with fresh water plus 2 inches. cook until chickpeas are very soft so you can easily squeeze them with two fingers. takes about 20-30 min. during cooking remove foam and any shells that float on top.
- retain a cup of cooked chickpeas on the side for garnish. also retain 2 cups of the cooking water.
- let the pot cool down for about 30 min. discard of the water and the garlic.
- place the peas in a food processor and grind them for 1-2 min until mashed. add tahina and 1/4 cup of the lemon juice. process until its texture becomes smooth. slowly add 1/2 cup of the cooking water while continue to process.
- add cooking water, lemon juice and salt as needed until you reach your desired velvety texture and taste.
- place on a plate or a small bowl. garnish with cooked chickpeas, paprika, cumin and chopped parsley.

If frozen chickpeas are not available, those from a can will be good as well. Note those are a little salty

Onion and Tomatoes Salad

Don't like eating raw onion, no worries. This onion is cured in the lemon juice and salt, and you end up with a totally different experience. A must try.

What you need:

1 large red onion
1 lemon
4 tomatoes
4 Tbsp olive oil
salt and pepper

Great Additions:
* *kalamata olives*
* *parsley or coriander*

What will you need to do:

- cut onion into half longwise. slice the onion as thin as possible (1/16 inch (1-2 mm) or thinner, it will not work on thicker slices). separate the layers so you get thin strings. place in a large mixing bowl.
- squeeze the entire lemon into the bowl, add 4 Tbsp of olive oil and 1 tsp of salt (looks a lot but this is all the salt you need for this salad).
- mix well, and let sit for at least half an hour, the more the merrier (up to an hour). every 10 min. mix well make sure all the onion is well covered with the liquids.
- Slice the tomatoes, or cut into large cubes. add to the bowl with all their juices. mix well. let the salad sit for another 10 min. before serving.
- taste. add olive oil, salt, lemon and a pinch of pepper if needed.

Half Blooded Potatoes

These potatoes are like french fries, but without the deep fry. Inside is soft and buttery and shell is crisp. What is also great about these potatoes is that you can add different flavors to make them suit your audience.

What you need:

6-8 medium potatoes
6 Tbsp olive oil
coarse salt

What you need to do:

- put the potatoes, skin on, in a pot. cover with water and cook for about 7-10 min. after water are boiling (potatoes should be cooked but still be firmed for a touch).
- remove all cooking water and let the potatoes cool down (this will make them cooked all the way).
- skin off. cut the potatoes into medium size cubes (each potato into 6 cubes).
- heat a skillet.
- add 2 Tbsp of oil. add a pinch of coarse salt into the oil. add 1/3 of the potatoes cubes (or enough to cover the skillet in one layer) and saute until golden brown, turning every couple of minutes to brown at least couple of sides. remove to a serving dish. repeat to saute all the potatoes.
- in the last batch add back all the already cooked potatoes to reheat before serving.

Add fresh herbs like thyme, chopped rosemary leaves or oregano right at the end of sautéing

Grilled Eggplants

Eggplants might not be favorite food by kids, but Hi! grownups need to eat good too.
This is a wonderful way to prepare eggplants (best is to grill them right over your stove or BBQ).

Since the cooking itself is so straightforward, it is all about what goes around it.

What you need:

2 medium size eggplants
2 Tbsp olive oil
coarse salt

Replace the olive oil with Thina (make it a little more liquidly for dressing).

* Thina recipe on page 26.

What you need to do:

- preheat oven to 400F (200C).
- cover a baking sheet with parchment
  paper. place eggplants in the oven for about 20-30 min.
- remove from the oven and let cool down for few minutes.
- place on a plate and cut them length wise. sprinkle some salt and drizzle 1/2 Tbsp of olive oil
  on each side of an eggplant.

Make it in a bowl:
After slicing the eggplants, scoop the flesh out into a ball. Add 1 clove of minced garlic. Add 2 Tbsp of olive oil and salt. mix well and serve.

 * little pieces of eggplant skin in the bowl will give it a
smoky flavor

Red Fruit Crumbles

The easiest desert ever made, but what a wonderful taste and beauty with the red breaking between the crumbles.

What you need:

Crumbles:
1 cup flour
4 oz (100 gr) butter
6 Tbsp sugar
pinch of salt

Fruit:
1 lb (1/2 kg) mixture of fruits
3 Tbsp sugar

Red fruits are great, other type of fruits are also welcome, like Apples or Pears

It's also very easy to make the crumbles with your hands. Kids will love preparing it.

What you need to do:

- preheat the oven to 400F (200C).
- in a food processor work all crumbles ingredients until it becomes like breadcrumbs.
- put the fruits in an ovenproof serving dish or small personal serving dishes, sprinkle with sugar. spread the crumbles over. shake it to avoid holes add crumbles where necessary.
- bake for 1/2 an hour or until the crumbles crust is golden.
- remove from the oven and let cool down as the fruits are boiling hot!

Chocolate Lava Personal Cake

The desert that will always makes people happy. Once you see the chocolate running downstream on the plate you just can't hold that smile from showing.
Remember this magic is all about timing.

What you need:

7 oz (200 gr) bitter-sweet chocolate
7 oz (200 gr) butter
2 eggs
2 egg yolks
4 Tbsp sugar
3 Tbsp flour

Write your baking time here:

_____

What you need to do:

- preheat the oven to 360F (180C).
- put chocolate and butter in a mixing bowl and melt them in the microwave (2-3 30 sec. intervals will do the trick) and mix well until mixture is uniform and liquid.
- mix in the 2 whole eggs until they incorporate.
- mix the 2 egg yolks and work them until completely incorporate.
- add sugar and a pinch of salt. mix well.
- sift in the flour. fold the flour into the mixture with a spatula (minimum folding moves).
- pour the mixture into a muffin pan (should fit a 6 holes pan).
- bake until cakes are NEARLY done, 7-12 min. time it!
- release the cakes from the sides using a knife, and let it cool a little inside the pan.
- using a large flat plate or a cutting board flip the cakes out of the baking pan.
- use a wide spatula or a wide chef knife to place each cake on a serving plate.
- serve hot.

NEARLY means:
Baked with a unbaked small center.

notes

notes

notes